SMUCKER'S
Best-Loved
RECIPES

SMUCKER'S®
Best-Loved
RECIPES

Publications International, Ltd.

Favorite Brand Name Recipes at www.fbnr.com

Microwave Cooking: Microwave ovens vary in wattage. Use the cooking times as guidelines and check for doneness before adding more time.

contents

A World of Potential...
Right in Your Own Cupboard

What do you get when you put Jif® peanut butter and Smucker's® jelly together? The answer is a winning combination for making tasty and satisfying meals for the entire family. Although the best-known combination is a peanut butter and jelly sandwich, there are a myriad of ways to incorporate the popular pair into recipes for breakfast, snacks, lunch, dinner, and dessert. This cookbook illustrates how Jif® peanut butter can be transformed into an Asian dipping sauce for grilled chicken, a moist coffee cake, and a refreshing ice cream shake. You'll also discover that Smucker's® jams, jellies, and preserves can be used as key ingredients for entrées such as Glazed Pork Chops, Peach-Pepper Chicken, and Sautéed Swordfish with Cherry Salsa. Finally, there is a special chapter for after-school snacks including prize-winning recipes from children who shared their favorite ways to use Jif® peanut butter in creative, yummy sandwiches. We hope this sampling of dishes using Jif® and Smucker's® highlights the versatility of our products and encourages you to cook these easy, delicious, and wholesome recipes for the entire family.

For more than 100 years, The J.M. Smucker Company has been a family-run business committed to using the highest quality ingredients in every jar. Back in 1897, in the Midwestern farming community of Orrville, Ohio, Jerome Monroe Smucker pressed locally grown apples into cider and apple butter. True to his upbringing, Jerome took great pride in a job well done and signed the lid of every crock of apple butter as his personal guarantee of quality. By adhering to a very simple set of Basic Beliefs, The J.M. Smucker Company grew and prospered. Today, more than a century later, the company is the market leader in fruit spreads, ice cream toppings, health and natural foods and beverages, and natural peanut butter in North America. In 2002, the company further enhanced its leadership position with the addition of Jif® peanut butter and CRISCO® shortening and oils to the Smucker family of brands.

The addition of Jif® peanut butter expands our tradition of providing high-quality, great-tasting foods for you and your family. Jif® peanut butter has been a favorite for generations and earned its reputation for having the most fresh roasted peanut taste of any leading creamy peanut butter. In fact, each 28-ounce jar of Jif® peanut butter contains approximately 1,218 peanuts. To keep up with America's love for peanut butter, the Jif® plant, located in Lexington, Kentucky, is the largest peanut butter factory in the world. We are proud to manufacture a nutritious product that supplies protein, minerals, and vitamins that the whole family can enjoy.

Be sure to read our helpful "Tips" for ways to modify dishes so that you have the flexibility to choose your favorite flavors. To find even more recipes using Jif® peanut butter and Smucker's® products, check out our websites: www.jif.com and www.smuckers.com. Both sites have product information, fun facts, and news about upcoming contests or events. Who knew America's favorite sandwich combination could be enjoyed at every mealtime!

rise and shine
BREAKFASTS

breakfast blossoms

1 (12-ounce) can buttermilk biscuits (10 biscuits)
¾ cup SMUCKER'S® Strawberry Preserves
¼ teaspoon ground cinnamon
¼ teaspoon ground nutmeg

1. Preheat oven to 375°F. Grease 10 (2½- or 3-inch) muffin pan cups. Separate dough into 10 biscuits. Separate each biscuit into 3 equal sections or leaves. For each blossom, stand 3 sections evenly around side and bottom of cup, overlapping slightly. Press dough edges firmly together.

2. Combine preserves, cinnamon and nutmeg in small bowl; stir until well blended. Place 1 tablespoon preserves mixture in center of each cup.

3. Bake at 375°F for 10 to 12 minutes or until lightly browned. Cool slightly before removing from pan. Serve warm. *Makes 10 rolls*

BREAKFASTS

peanut butter coffee cake

1½ cups packed brown sugar, divided
2½ cups PILLSBURY BEST® All-Purpose Flour, divided
¾ cup JIF® Creamy Peanut Butter, divided
2 tablespoons butter or margarine, melted
¼ cup CRISCO® Shortening
2 eggs
2 teaspoons baking powder
½ teaspoon salt
½ teaspoon baking soda
1 cup milk
Powdered sugar icing (optional)

1. Preheat oven to 375°F. Lightly grease 13×9×2-inch baking pan.

2. For topping, combine ½ cup brown sugar, ½ cup flour, ¼ cup peanut butter and melted butter in small bowl until crumbly; set aside.

3. Combine remaining ½ cup peanut butter and ¼ cup shortening in large bowl; beat until well blended. Gradually beat in remaining 1 cup brown sugar. Add eggs, 1 at a time, beating until fluffy.

4. Combine remaining 2 cups flour, baking powder, salt and baking soda in medium bowl; mix well. Add flour mixture alternately with milk to creamed mixture, beating after each addition.

5. Spread batter in prepared pan. Sprinkle with topping. Bake at 375°F for 30 to 35 minutes or until toothpick inserted into center comes out clean. Cool completely. Drizzle with icing, if desired.

Makes 16 to 18 servings

Pillsbury Best is a trademark of The Pillsbury Company, used under license.

peanut butter coffee cake

BREAKFASTS

apricot-peanut butter muffins

1¾ cups PILLSBURY BEST® All-Purpose or Unbleached Flour
2½ tablespoons sugar
2½ teaspoons baking powder
¾ teaspoon salt
¼ cup CRISCO® Shortening
¼ cup JIF® Creamy Peanut Butter
¾ cup milk
2 eggs
2 tablespoons SMUCKER'S® Apricot Preserves

1. Preheat oven to 400°F. Grease 10 large muffin pan cups.

2. Combine flour, sugar, baking powder and salt in large bowl; cut in ¼ cup shortening and peanut butter with pastry blender or 2 knives.

3. Combine milk and eggs in small bowl; add all at once to dry ingredients. Stir just until dry ingredients are moistened.

4. Fill muffin cups ⅔ full. Spoon about ½ teaspoon preserves into center of each muffin.

5. Bake at 400°F for 25 minutes or until toothpick inserted near centers comes out clean.   *Makes 10 muffins*

Pillsbury Best is a trademark of The Pillsbury Company, used under license.

Tip

Substitute your favorite Smucker's® flavor in place of the apricot preserves in the above recipe. Experiment with strawberry, blackberry, or even apple butter.

BREAKFASTS

breakfast popover

POPOVER
 ½ cup PILLSBURY BEST® All-Purpose Flour
 ½ cup skim milk
 4 egg whites
 1 tablespoon butter or margarine, melted
 ⅛ teaspoon salt

TOPPING
 1½ cups chopped apples
 ½ cup SMUCKER'S® Apple Jelly
 2 tablespoons water
 ⅛ teaspoon ground cinnamon

1. Preheat oven to 400°F. Coat 8-inch square baking pan with nonstick cooking spray.

2. Combine flour and milk in medium bowl; whisk until well blended. Whisk in egg whites, butter and salt. Pour into prepared pan. Bake at 400°F for 25 to 30 minutes or until puffed and golden brown.

3. Meanwhile, combine all topping ingredients in small saucepan; cook over low heat until apples are tender and mixture is hot, stirring frequently.

4. Immediately after removing popover from oven, cut into fourths and serve with hot topping.   *Makes 4 servings*

Variation: When in season, strawberries, blackberries, and raspberries make a delicious substitution for the apples in the above recipe. Make sure to also use a complementary flavored jelly in the topping.

Pillsbury Best is a trademark of The Pillsbury Company, used under license.

BREAKFASTS

stuffed french toast

1 (8-ounce) package cream cheese, softened
2 tablespoons sugar
1½ teaspoons vanilla, divided
¼ teaspoon ground cinnamon
½ cup chopped walnuts or pecans
1 (1-pound) loaf French bread
4 egg whites
1 cup whipping cream or half-and-half
½ teaspoon nutmeg
1 (12-ounce) jar SMUCKER'S® Apricot Preserves
½ cup orange juice
½ teaspoon almond extract
Fresh fruit

1. Combine cream cheese, sugar, 1 teaspoon vanilla and cinnamon in large bowl; beat until fluffy. Stir in nuts; set aside.

2. Cut bread into 10 to 12 (1½- to 2-inch) slices; cut pocket in top of each slice. Fill each pocket with about 1½ tablespoons cream cheese mixture.

3. Combine egg whites, whipping cream, remaining ½ teaspoon vanilla and nutmeg in large bowl; beat until well blended. Using tongs, dip bread slices in egg mixture, being careful not to squeeze out filling. Cook on lightly greased griddle until both sides are golden brown. (To keep cooked slices hot for serving, place on baking sheet in 200°F oven.)

4. Meanwhile, combine preserves and orange juice in microwave-safe bowl; heat in microwave until warm. Stir in almond extract. To serve, drizzle apricot mixture over French toast. Serve with fresh fruit.

Makes 10 to 12 slices

stuffed french toast

BREAKFASTS

orange marmalade bread

3 cups PILLSBURY BEST® All-Purpose or Unbleached Flour
4 teaspoons baking powder
1 teaspoon salt
½ cup chopped walnuts
¾ cup milk
¾ cup SMUCKER'S® Sweet Orange Marmalade
2 eggs, lightly beaten
¼ cup honey
2 tablespoons CRISCO® Oil*

*Use your favorite Crisco Oil.

1. Preheat oven to 350°F. Grease 9×5×3-inch loaf pan. Combine flour, baking powder and salt in large bowl. Stir in nuts. Combine milk, marmalade, eggs, honey and oil in medium bowl; stir until well blended. Add marmalade mixture to flour mixture; stir just until dry ingredients are moistened. (Batter will be lumpy.) Turn into prepared pan.

2. Bake at 350°F for 65 to 70 minutes or until lightly browned and toothpick inserted into center comes out clean.

Makes 8 to 10 servings

Pillsbury Best is a trademark of The Pillsbury Company, used under license.

orange marmalade bread

BREAKFASTS

blueberry coffee cake

COFFEE CAKE
1½ cups PILLSBURY BEST® All-Purpose or Unbleached Flour, divided
¼ cup granulated sugar
2½ teaspoons baking powder
½ teaspoon salt
¼ teaspoon ground allspice
⅔ cup milk
⅓ cup butter or margarine, melted
1 egg
¾ cup SMUCKER'S® Blueberry Preserves

TOPPING
¼ cup firmly packed brown sugar
¼ cup chopped walnuts
2 tablespoons PILLSBURY BEST® All-Purpose or Unbleached Flour
1 tablespoon butter or margarine

1. Preheat oven to 400°F. Grease and flour 8- or 9-inch square baking pan.

2. Combine 1 cup flour, granulated sugar, baking powder, salt and allspice in medium bowl. Add milk, melted butter and egg; stir vigorously until well blended.

3. Pour half of batter into prepared pan; spread preserves evenly over batter. Top with remaining batter.

4. Combine all topping ingredients in small bowl; stir until crumbly. Sprinkle over batter in pan.

5. Bake at 400°F for 20 to 25 minutes or until toothpick inserted into center comes out clean.   *Makes 9 servings*

Pillsbury Best is a trademark of The Pillsbury Company, used under license.

raspberry breakfast braid

BRAID
    2 cups packaged baking mix
    1 (3-ounce) package cream cheese
    ¼ cup butter or margarine
    ⅓ cup milk
    ½ cup SMUCKER'S® Red Raspberry Preserves

GLAZE
    1 cup powdered sugar
    ¼ teaspoon almond extract
    ¼ teaspoon vanilla
    1 to 2 tablespoons milk

1. Preheat oven to 425°F. Place baking mix in medium bowl. Cut in cream cheese and butter until mixture is crumbly. Stir in milk. Turn dough out onto lightly floured surface and knead lightly 10 to 12 times.

2. Roll dough into 12×8-inch rectangle. Transfer to greased baking sheet. Spread preserves lengthwise down center ⅓ of dough. Make 2½-inch cuts at 1-inch intervals on long sides. Fold strips over filling.

3. Bake at 425°F for 12 to 15 minutes or until lightly browned.

4. Combine all glaze ingredients in small bowl, adding enough milk for desired drizzling consistency. Drizzle over coffeecake.

Makes 10 to 12 servings

lively LUNCHES

smucker's® three bean salad with sweet and sour apricot dressing

½ cup **SMUCKER'S® Apricot Preserves**
¼ cup **red wine vinegar**
 1 teaspoon **celery seeds**
 1 (16-ounce) can **kidney beans, rinsed and drained**
¼ pound (1 cup) **cooked fresh or frozen green beans,**
     cut into 2-inch pieces
¼ pound (1 cup) **cooked fresh or frozen yellow wax**
     beans, cut into 2-inch pieces
 1 small **red onion, thinly sliced**
    Salt and black pepper to taste

1. Combine preserves, vinegar and celery seeds in medium salad bowl; stir until well blended.

2. Add kidney beans, green and yellow beans and onion. Toss well to blend. Season with salt and freshly ground black pepper.   *Makes 6 servings*

LUNCHES

broccoli noodle salad with asian peanut citrus sauce

1 pound thin spaghetti
½ cup plus 1 teaspoon CRISCO® Canola Oil,* divided
½ cup JIF® Creamy Peanut Butter
½ cup orange juice
½ cup lemon juice
½ cup soy sauce
1 tablespoon sugar
1 cup chopped onion
½ cup chopped red, yellow or green bell pepper, or any combination of bell peppers
1 to 2 tablespoons minced garlic
1 pound broccoli florets

Or use your favorite Crisco Oil.

1. Cook spaghetti according to package directions; drain well. Place in large bowl; toss with 1 teaspoon oil. Set aside.

2. For Asian Peanut Citrus Sauce, combine peanut butter, orange juice, lemon juice, soy sauce and sugar in medium bowl. Whisk until very well blended.

3. Heat remaining ½ cup oil in large, deep skillet over medium heat. Add onion, bell pepper and garlic; cook and stir about 1 minute. Stir in broccoli. Add Asian Peanut Citrus Sauce; cook and stir until broccoli is crisp-tender.

4. Toss broccoli mixture with spaghetti. Serve at room temperature. Store salad covered in refrigerator for up to 2 days.   *Makes 6 servings*

broccoli noodle salad with asian peanut citrus sauce

LUNCHES

waldorf salad with turkey and apricot

DRESSING
½ cup nonfat plain yogurt
⅓ cup SMUCKER'S® Apricot Preserves
2 tablespoons lemon juice
1 teaspoon dried tarragon, chives, parsley or curry powder
1 teaspoon Dijon mustard
½ teaspoon salt
½ teaspoon grated lemon peel
⅛ teaspoon freshly ground black pepper

SALAD
1 pound boneless skinless turkey or chicken, cooked and cubed*
1 cup diced unpeeled red apple (½-inch pieces)
1 cup diced unpeeled green apple (½-inch pieces)
1 cup diced celery (¼-inch pieces)
¼ cup raisins
4 lettuce leaves
1 tablespoon chopped fresh parsley or chives

Deli turkey breast may be used in the recipe. Ask the deli to slice the turkey into ¾- or 1-inch slices, then cube the meat at home before adding to this salad.

1. Combine all dressing ingredients in small bowl; stir until well blended. Add turkey, apples, celery and raisins. Toss to coat. Season with additional salt and pepper, if desired.

2. Place lettuce leaf on each of 4 serving plates. Top each with mound of salad. Garnish each salad with chopped fresh parsley or chives.

Makes 4 servings

waldorf salad with turkey and apricot

LUNCHES

smoked turkey and strawberry spinach salad

DRESSING
- ½ cup SMUCKER'S® Strawberry Jelly
- 2 tablespoons red wine vinegar
- 2 teaspoons grated lemon peel

SALAD
- 4 cups baby spinach
- 2 cups cubed cooked smoked turkey or chicken
- 1⅓ cups sliced or halved fresh strawberries
- 1 (11-ounce) can mandarin oranges, chilled and drained
- 2 thin slices red onion, separated into rings

1. Combine jelly, vinegar and lemon peel in small saucepan. Cook over medium-high heat until jelly is melted, stirring frequently. Cool 10 minutes.

2. Meanwhile, arrange spinach, turkey, strawberries, oranges and onion rings on 4 individual salad plates. Serve with dressing.

Makes 4 servings

Tip

For a delicious alternative, substitute ½ cup Smucker's® Red Raspberry Preserves for the jelly and 1½ cups fresh raspberries for the strawberries in the above recipe.

smoked turkey and strawberry spinach salad

LUNCHES

peanut butter and jelly pizza sandwich

   1 English muffin
   2 tablespoons JIF® Creamy Peanut Butter
   2 tablespoons SMUCKER'S® Strawberry Preserves
   6 to 8 slices banana
      Chocolate syrup
      Sweetened flaked coconut (optional)

1. Split and toast English muffin. Spread peanut butter on both halves of English muffin. Spread preserves over peanut butter.

2. Top with banana slices. Drizzle with chocolate syrup to taste. Sprinkle with coconut flakes, if desired. Serve warm.   *Makes 1 serving*

peanut butter and jelly club sandwich

   3 tablespoons JIF® Creamy Peanut Butter
   3 slices bread
   2 tablespoons SMUCKER'S® Strawberry Jam
   ½ banana, sliced
   2 strawberries, sliced

1. Spread peanut butter on 2 slices of bread. Spread jam on remaining slice of bread.

2. Place sliced banana on top of 1 slice of bread with peanut butter. Place sliced strawberries on top of other piece of bread with peanut butter.

3. Place piece of bread with strawberries on top of bread with bananas. Close sandwich with slice of bread with jam facing down.

Makes 1 serving

peanut butter and jelly pizza sandwich

after-school
SNACKS

candied spiced mixed nuts

---

  8 cups salted mixed nuts
  2 teaspoons CRISCO® Oil*
1⅓ cups SMUCKER'S® Strawberry Jelly
  4 tablespoons plus 2 teaspoons paprika, divided
  6 teaspoons cumin, divided
  1 cup brown sugar

*Use your favorite Crisco Oil.

1. Combine nuts and oil in medium bowl; toss to coat. Set aside.

2. Melt jelly in small saucepan over medium heat. Add 4 tablespoons paprika and 4 teaspoons cumin; stir until well blended. Cook to hard ball stage, 260°F measured on candy thermometer (or test for hard ball stage by dropping small amount of mixture into glass of ice water; mixture will harden instantly if it has reached proper temperature).

3. Immediately pour mixture over nuts. Stir with wooden spoon to evenly coat. Cool for 5 minutes.

4. Combine brown sugar, remaining 2 teaspoons paprika and remaining 2 teaspoons cumin in small bowl. When cool enough to handle, sprinkle nuts with brown sugar mixture. Let cool completely.   *Makes 8 cups nuts*

SNACKS

sweet and sour hot dog bites

½ cup SMUCKER'S® Concord Grape Jelly
¼ cup prepared mustard
1 tablespoon sweet pickle relish
½ pound frankfurters, cooked

1. Combine jelly, mustard and relish in small saucepan. Heat over very low heat, stirring constantly, until mixture is hot and well blended.

2. Slice frankfurters diagonally into bite-size pieces. Add to sauce and heat thoroughly. *Makes 20 snack servings*

chunky raspberry applesauce

4 apples, peeled, cored and quartered
¾ cup raspberry or raspberry blend juice
¾ teaspoon ground cinnamon
6 tablespoons SMUCKER'S® Raspberry Preserves

1. Combine apples, raspberry juice and cinnamon in medium saucepan. Bring to a boil. Reduce heat; cover and simmer for 20 minutes, stirring occasionally, until apples are tender when pierced with fork.

2. Melt preserves in small saucepan or microwave in small, microwave-safe bowl. Strain to remove seeds; set aside.

3. Beat apple mixture lightly with electric mixer to form chunky sauce. Stir in preserves.

4. Serve applesauce warm, or cover and refrigerate until serving time.

Makes 3½ cups applesauce

sweet and sour hot dog bites

SNACKS

double peanut snack mix

    4 cups sweet shredded oat cereal
    1 cup peanuts
    ½ cup butter or margarine
    ½ cup JIF® Creamy Peanut Butter
    1 teaspoon ground cinnamon

1. Preheat oven to 350°F. Combine cereal and peanuts in large bowl.

2. Heat butter, peanut butter and cinnamon in small saucepan over low heat until butter and peanut butter are melted. Stir until well blended.

3. Slowly pour peanut butter mixture over cereal mixture; mix well. Spread into 13×9×2-inch baking pan.

4. Bake at 350°F for 10 to 12 minutes, stirring occasionally. Cool.

Makes 4 cups snack mix

trail mix bars

    3 cups crispy rice cereal
    3 cups toasted oat cereal
1½ cups raisins
    ½ cup sunflower seeds
    1 cup honey
    ¾ cup sugar
    1 (18-ounce) jar JIF® Extra Crunchy Peanut Butter
    1 teaspoon vanilla

1. Combine cereals, raisins and sunflower seeds in large bowl.

2. Combine honey and sugar in medium saucepan; heat over medium heat for 3 to 5 minutes or until mixture comes to a boil. Boil for 1 minute.

3. Add peanut butter and vanilla; stir until peanut butter is melted. Pour over cereal mixture; mix well.

4. Press mixture into greased 15×10×1-inch baking pan. Cool completely. Cut into 1½-inch bars.

Makes 1 dozen bars

double peanut snack mix

SNACKS

buckeye balls

1 ½ cups JIF® Creamy Peanut Butter
½ cup butter or margarine, softened
1 teaspoon vanilla
½ teaspoon salt
3 to 4 cups powdered sugar

COATING
1 pound chocolate flavored candy coating
2 tablespoons CRISCO® Shortening

1. Combine peanut butter, butter, vanilla and salt in large bowl. Beat at low speed of electric mixer until blended. Add 2 cups powdered sugar. Beat until blended. Continue adding sugar, ½ cup at a time, until mixture can be shaped into ball that will hold together on toothpick. Shape into ¾-inch balls. Place on waxed paper-lined baking sheet. Refrigerate.

2. For coating, combine candy coating and shortening in microwave-safe bowl. Microwave at 50% (MEDIUM) for 30 seconds. Stir. Repeat until mixture is smooth.

3. For each candy, insert toothpick into peanut butter ball. Dip about ¾ of ball into melted coating; scrape off excess. Place on waxed paper-lined baking sheet. Remove toothpick; smooth over hole. Refrigerate until coating is firm; remove from paper. Store at room temperature in covered container. *Makes 8 dozen candies*

buckeye balls

SNACKS

peanut butter shakes

1 cup cold milk
¼ cup JIF® Creamy Peanut Butter
1 cup vanilla ice cream
Whipped cream and chopped peanuts (optional)

1. Place milk and peanut butter in blender container. Cover and blend until smooth. Add ice cream; blend until smooth.

2. Divide shake between 2 glasses. Top with whipped cream and sprinkle with chopped nuts, if desired.   *Makes 2 servings*

Variation: For Banana JIF® Shakes, prepare recipe as directed above, except add a sliced banana to the blender container with the JIF® peanut butter.

haystacks

2 cups butterscotch chips
½ cup JIF® Creamy Peanut Butter
¼ CRISCO® Butter Flavor Stick or ¼ cup CRISCO® Butter Flavor
    Shortening
6 cups corn flakes
⅔ cup miniature semisweet chocolate chips
Chopped peanuts or chocolate jimmies (optional)

1. Combine butterscotch chips, peanut butter and ¼ cup shortening in large microwave-safe bowl. Cover with waxed paper. Microwave at 50% (MEDIUM). Stir after 1 minute. Repeat until smooth. (Or melt on rangetop in small saucepan over very low heat, stirring constantly.)

2. Pour corn flakes into large bowl. Pour hot butterscotch mixture over flakes. Stir with spoon until flakes are coated. Stir in chocolate chips.

3. Spoon ½ cup mixture into mounds on waxed paper-lined baking sheets. Sprinkle with chopped nuts, if desired. Refrigerate until firm.

Makes 3 dozen cookies

peanut butter shake

SNACKS

topping for frozen yogurt or ice cream

**¼ cup pancake syrup
3 tablespoons Reduced Fat JIF® Crunchy or Creamy Peanut Butter**

1. Combine syrup and peanut butter in microwave-safe measuring cup.

2. Microwave at 50% (MEDIUM) for 30 seconds. Stir. Repeat until smooth. Cool slightly.

3. Pour warm sauce over frozen yogurt or ice cream.

Makes ½ cup topping

Tip: If topping becomes too thick, thin with a little additional syrup.

Tip

Make sure to try all of Smucker's® Toppings to garnish your favorite ice cream flavor. Smucker's® offers a range of flavors such as hot fudge, butterscotch and dulce de leche.

SNACKS

pb & j pinwheels

1 CRISCO® Butter Flavor Stick or 1 cup CRISCO® Butter Flavor
   Shortening
1 cup JIF® Creamy Peanut Butter
¾ cup granulated sugar
¾ cup firmly packed light brown sugar
2 eggs
1 teaspoon vanilla
2½ cups PILLSBURY BEST® All-Purpose or Unbleached Flour
1 teaspoon salt
1 teaspoon baking soda
½ cup SMUCKER'S® Seedless Red Raspberry Jam
⅔ cup very finely chopped peanuts
   CRISCO® No-Stick Cooking Spray
   Additional SMUCKER'S® Seedless Red Raspberry Jam (optional)

1. Combine shortening, peanut butter, granulated sugar and brown sugar in large bowl. Beat at medium speed of electric mixer until well blended. Beat in eggs and vanilla.

2. Combine flour, salt and baking soda. Add gradually to creamed mixture at low speed. Beat until well blended.

3. Cut parchment paper to line 17×11-inch baking pan. Press dough out to edges of paper. Spread with jam to within ½ inch of edges.

4. Lift up long side of paper. Loosen dough with spatula. Roll dough up jelly-roll fashion. Seal seam. Sprinkle nuts on paper. Roll dough over nuts. Press on any extra nuts. Wrap in plastic wrap. Place in plastic bag. Refrigerate overnight.

5. Preheat oven to 375° F. Spray baking sheet with cooking spray. Unwrap dough; cut into ½-inch slices. Place slices 2 inches apart on prepared baking sheet.

6. Bake at 375°F for 10 to 12 minutes or until set. Cool about 5 minutes on baking sheet before removing to cooling rack. Top with additional jam before serving, if desired.   *Makes about 3 dozen cookies*

Pillsbury Best is a trademark of The Pillsbury Company, used under license.

SNACKS

cheese tortellini twirls with peach sauce

2 (9-ounce) packages fresh cheese tortellini
1 cup (12-ounce jar) SMUCKER'S® Peach Preserves
½ cup diced black olives
¼ cup red vinegar
2 tablespoons tomato paste
1 teaspoon chopped garlic
¼ teaspoon black pepper
¼ cup chopped fresh parsley or basil

1. Cook tortellini according to package directions.

2. Thread 3 tortellini onto each of 16 skewers. Place in shallow baking dish.

3. Combine all remaining ingredients except parsley; pour over tortellini. Cover with plastic wrap and marinate overnight in refrigerator.

4. Serve tortellini cold or bake at 350°F for 12 to 15 minutes. Serve garnished with parsley.   *Makes 16 kabobs*

peanut butter and oats bars

 1 cup firmly packed dark brown sugar
 ¾ CRISCO® Butter Flavor Stick or ¾ cup CRISCO® Butter Flavor
    Shortening plus additional for greasing
 ½ cup JIF® Creamy Peanut Butter
 2 cups plus 2 tablespoons PILLSBURY BEST® All-Purpose Flour
 1 teaspoon salt
 ½ teaspoon baking soda
1½ cups oats (quick, uncooked)
 ⅓ cup water
 1 cup SMUCKER'S® Strawberry Preserves

1. Preheat oven to 400°F. Grease 13×9×2-inch baking pan with shortening.

2. Combine brown sugar, shortening and peanut butter in large bowl. Beat at medium speed of electric mixer until well blended.

3. Combine flour, salt and baking soda in medium bowl. Add gradually to creamed mixture at low speed. Beat until well blended. Stir in oats with spoon. Mix until well blended. Stir in water 1 tablespoon at a time.

4. Press half the dough onto bottom of prepared pan; spread preserves over dough. Flatten small amounts of remaining dough between hands. Place on preserves and arrange so dough sections touch. Fill in any spaces with dough so preserves are completely covered.

5. Bake at 400°F for 25 to 30 minutes or until edges are golden brown. Do not overbake. Cut into 2¼×2-inch bars while warm.

Makes 2 dozen bars

Pillsbury Best is a trademark of The Pillsbury Company, used under license.

school-night SUPPERS

peach-pepper chicken

---

1 (4-pound) broiler chicken, cut into serving pieces
½ teaspoon salt
¼ cup butter or margarine
¾ cup SMUCKER'S® Peach Preserves
1 medium onion, sliced
1 medium green or red bell pepper, cut into strips
1 tablespoon lemon juice
½ teaspoon ground ginger
1 teaspoon cornstarch
2 tablespoons water

1. Sprinkle chicken with salt. Melt butter in large skillet. Add chicken pieces and brown lightly on all sides.

2. Combine preserves, onion, bell pepper, lemon juice and ginger in medium bowl; stir until well blended. Pour over chicken; cover and simmer for 25 minutes.

3. Blend cornstarch with water in small bowl. Stir into sauce; cook until sauce is slightly thickened. Serve with rice. *Makes 4 servings*

SUPPERS

glazed pork chops

6 pork loin or rib chops, ¾ inch thick
1 cup SMUCKER'S® Blackberry Jam
¾ cup ketchup
¼ cup steak sauce
1 teaspoon dry mustard
1 clove garlic, minced

1. Preheat broiler. Broil pork chops 3 to 5 inches from heat for 5 minutes. Turn; broil 5 minutes longer.

2. Meanwhile, combine remaining ingredients in small saucepan. Heat over medium-high heat to boiling; simmer over low heat for 10 minutes.

3. Brush pork with sauce. Continue broiling, turning and brushing with sauce, 5 to 10 minutes longer, or until pork is no longer pink in center. Bring remaining sauce to a boil; boil for 1 minute. Serve sauce with pork chops.   *Makes 6 servings*

glazed pork chop

SUPPERS

grilled chicken breasts with zesty peanut sauce

8 large boneless skinless chicken breast halves

MARINADE
½ cup soy sauce
⅓ cup fresh lime juice
¼ cup CRISCO® All-Vegetable Oil*
2 tablespoons JIF® Creamy or Extra Crunchy Peanut Butter
1 tablespoon brown sugar
2 large cloves garlic, minced
½ teaspoon salt
½ teaspoon cayenne pepper

SAUCE
1 cup JIF® Creamy or Extra Crunchy Peanut Butter
1 cup unsweetened coconut milk
¼ cup fresh lime juice
3 tablespoons soy sauce
2 tablespoons dark brown sugar
2 teaspoons minced fresh ginger
2 cloves garlic, minced
¼ teaspoon cayenne pepper, or to taste
½ cup chicken broth
½ cup heavy cream

Or use your favorite Crisco Oil.

1. Rinse, trim and pound chicken to ¼-inch thickness. Combine chicken and all marinade ingredients in resealable plastic food storage bag. Marinate for 1 hour or overnight in refrigerator.

2. Combine first 8 sauce ingredients in medium saucepan over medium heat. Cook for 15 minutes, stirring constantly. Whisk in broth and cream. Cook for 1 minute. Set aside.

3. Preheat grill. Remove chicken from marinade and place on hot grid. Grill for 4 to 6 minutes on each side or until center is no longer pink. Serve hot topped with peanut sauce.   *Makes 8 servings*

grilled chicken breasts with zesty peanut sauce

SUPPERS

baked ham with apple-raspberry sauce

1 (3-pound) canned ham
1 cup chopped green apples
½ cup SMUCKER'S® Red Raspberry Preserves
½ cup SMUCKER'S® Apple Jelly
¾ cup apple cider
1 tablespoon cider vinegar
2 tablespoons cornstarch
Endive or fresh parsley sprigs and whole crabapples for garnish

1. Bake ham according to package directions.

2. Combine chopped apples, preserves and jelly in medium saucepan; stir until well blended. Combine cider, vinegar and cornstarch in small bowl; stir into saucepan. Heat over medium-high heat until mixture is boiling; boil, stirring constantly, until thickened, about 1 minute.

3. Slice ham and arrange on platter; garnish with endive and crabapples. Serve with sauce.   *Makes 8 to 10 servings*

Tip

Fresh crabapples are too sour to eat out of hand, but the canned spiced varieties are delicious with pork and poultry.

baked ham with apple-raspberry sauce

peanut butter & apple stuffed pork chops

4 (¾-inch-thick) center cut pork chops, fat trimmed
½ cup finely chopped apple
1 large shallot, minced, or ¼ cup minced onion
¼ cup seasoned bread crumbs, toasted*
¼ cup JIF® Creamy Peanut Butter
   CRISCO® No-Stick Cooking Spray
½ cup SMUCKER'S® Apple or Currant Jelly, melted
   Salt and black pepper to taste

To toast bread crumbs, place crumbs on a foil-lined baking pan and bake in a 300°F oven (or toaster oven) for 3 to 5 minutes or until lightly browned.

1. Make a "pocket" in each pork chop with small knife by cutting horizontally from outside edge almost to bone.

2. Combine apple, shallot, bread crumbs and peanut butter in medium bowl; mix well. Shape stuffing mixture into four equal patties.

3. Place one stuffing patty into each pork chop pocket. Using wooden toothpicks (2 to 3 per chop), close each pocket to prevent stuffing from falling out during cooking.

4. Preheat oven to 450°F. Spray pork chops lightly with cooking spray. Place large, oven-proof frying pan over medium-high heat until hot. Place pork chops in pan and cook for about 8 minutes, turning once, or until well browned on both sides.

5. Remove pan from stove and place in hot oven to cook for another 20 minutes. Baste pork chops with melted jelly during last 5 minutes of cooking. When pork chops are done, remove toothpicks and season with salt and black pepper.   *Makes 4 servings*

peanut butter & apple stuffed pork chop

SUPPERS

almond-dusted strawberry balsamic chicken breasts

CRISCO® Butter Flavor No-Stick Cooking Spray
1 tablespoon CRISCO® Canola Oil*
4 boneless skinless chicken breast halves
½ teaspoon salt
¼ teaspoon black pepper
⅓ cup finely chopped unblanched almonds
¼ cup minced shallots or green onions
⅓ cup chicken broth
⅓ cup SMUCKER'S® Strawberry Preserves
3 tablespoons balsamic vinegar
1 tablespoon minced fresh rosemary or 1 teaspoon dried rosemary, crumbled
1 (10-ounce) bag ready-to-serve fresh spinach, cooked just until tender and kept warm
Finely chopped fresh parsley for garnish (optional)

Or use your favorite Crisco Oil.

1. Coat large nonstick skillet with cooking spray; add oil and heat over medium-high heat. Sprinkle chicken with salt and pepper; dredge in almonds.

2. Place chicken in skillet; sauté for 4 minutes on each side. Remove from pan and keep warm.

3. Reduce heat to low. Add shallots to skillet; sauté for 1 minute. Add chicken broth, preserves, vinegar and rosemary; simmer until slightly thickened, about 2 to 3 minutes.

4. Place spinach on warm serving platter. Place chicken breasts on spinach; drizzle with sauce. Sprinkle finely chopped parsley over chicken, if desired. *Makes 4 servings*

apricot-glazed spareribs

6 pounds pork spareribs, cut into 2-rib portions
4 cloves garlic, crushed
  Water
1 (12-ounce) jar SMUCKER'S® Apricot Preserves
¼ cup chopped onion
¼ cup ketchup
2 tablespoons firmly packed brown sugar
1 tablespoon CRISCO® Vegetable Oil*
1 teaspoon soy sauce
1 teaspoon ground ginger
½ teaspoon salt

Or use your favorite Crisco Oil.

1. Combine pork spareribs and garlic in very large saucepot or Dutch oven; cover spareribs with water. Bring to a boil over high heat. Reduce heat to low; cover and simmer for 1 hour or until spareribs are fork-tender. Remove ribs to platter; cover and refrigerate.

2. Meanwhile for apricot glaze, combine preserves, onion, ketchup, brown sugar, oil, soy sauce, ginger and salt in small saucepan; mix well. Heat to boiling; boil 1 minute. Cover and refrigerate.

3. About 1 hour before serving, heat grill. When ready to barbecue, place cooked spareribs on grill over medium heat. Cook 12 to 15 minutes or until heated through, turning spareribs often. Brush occasionally with apricot glaze during last 10 minutes of cooking.   *Makes 6 servings*

Alternate Method: Precooked spareribs can be broiled in the oven. Place spareribs on broiler pan; brush with some apricot glaze. Broil about 7 to 9 inches from heat for 7 to 8 minutes, brushing with apricot glaze halfway through cooking time. Turn ribs; brush with apricot glaze and broil until meat is tender.

SUPPERS

mandarin shrimp & vegetable stir-fry

1 cup SMUCKER'S® Sweet Orange Marmalade
3 tablespoons soy sauce
2 tablespoons white vinegar
2 tablespoons hot pepper sauce
1½ tablespoons cornstarch
2 tablespoons CRISCO® All-Vegetable Oil*
1 tablespoon chopped fresh ginger
1 tablespoon chopped garlic
24 fresh uncooked large shrimp, peeled and deveined
1 red bell pepper, chopped
1 yellow or green bell pepper, chopped
3 cups broccoli florets
½ cup water
1 cup chopped green onions
Hot cooked rice (optional)

Or use your favorite Crisco Oil.

1. Combine marmalade, soy sauce, vinegar, hot pepper sauce and cornstarch in medium bowl; stir to dissolve cornstarch. Set aside.

2. Place large skillet or wok over high heat for 1 minute; add oil. Heat oil for 30 seconds; add ginger, garlic and shrimp. Stir-fry for 2 to 3 minutes or until shrimp turn rosy pink. Remove shrimp from pan; set aside.

3. Add bell peppers and broccoli to pan; cook over high heat for 1 minute. Add water; cover and reduce heat to medium. Cook for 4 to 5 minutes or until vegetables are tender.

4. Uncover pan and return heat to high. Add shrimp and marmalade mixture. Cook for another 2 minutes or until sauce is thickened and shrimp are completely cooked. Season with salt and freshly ground black pepper, if desired. Stir in green onions. Serve with hot cooked rice, if desired.   *Makes 4 to 6 servings*

mandarin shrimp & vegetable stir-fry

SUPPERS

peppered steak with blackberry sauce

⅓ cup lemon juice
⅓ cup CRISCO® Vegetable Oil*
¼ cup chopped onion
2 cloves garlic, minced
4 (4- to 6-ounce) beef tenderloin or eye of round steaks, trimmed
    of fat
1 tablespoon coarse ground black pepper
½ cup SMUCKER'S® Seedless Blackberry Jam
¼ cup red wine vinegar
¼ teaspoon onion powder
¼ cup fresh or thawed frozen blackberries

Or use your favorite Crisco Oil.

1. Combine lemon juice, oil, onion and garlic in large resealable plastic food storage bag; mix well. Place steaks in marinade. Seal bag; refrigerate for 6 to 24 hours, turning bag occasionally. When ready to cook, rub pepper around outside edges of each steak.

2. Preheat grill. Combine jam, vinegar and onion powder in small saucepan. Cook over medium heat until jam is melted, stirring constantly. Remove from heat.

3. Oil grill rack. Place steaks on gas grill over medium heat or on charcoal grill 4 to 6 inches from medium-high coals. Cook 8 to 12 minutes or until desired doneness, turning once halfway through cooking time. To serve, top steaks with blackberry sauce; sprinkle with fresh berries.   *Makes 4 servings*

Alternate method: Steaks can be cooked in the oven. Place on oiled broiler pan. Broil 4 to 7 inches from heat for 7 to 10 minutes or until desired doneness, turning once halfway through cooking time.

peppered steak with blackberry sauce

SUPPERS

grilled spicy red snapper with jamaican mango & peach relish

½ cup SMUCKER'S® Peach Preserves
    Juice of 1 lemon (about ⅓ cup)
1 small onion, finely chopped
1 teaspoon minced garlic
¼ teaspoon ground allspice
¼ teaspoon salt
¼ teaspoon freshly ground black pepper
1 large ripe mango, peeled and finely chopped
1 pound red snapper or swordfish fillets, cut into 4 portions
    Juice of 1 lime (about ⅓ cup)
½ teaspoon finely chopped hot chili pepper, or to taste
2 tablespoons chopped fresh parsley, chives or thyme (or a
    combination)
    Salt and black pepper to taste
2 tablespoons CRISCO® All-Vegetable Oil*

*Or use your favorite Crisco Oil.

1. Combine first 7 ingredients in medium bowl; mix well. Fold in mango. Cover with plastic wrap; refrigerate.

2. Using sharp knife, lightly score an "X" 3 to 4 times on 1 side of each fish fillet. Place fillets in shallow dish and rub with lime juice, hot pepper, herbs, salt and pepper. Refrigerate at least 1 hour or overnight.

3. Heat grill or broiler. Lightly oil fillets. Place on grill or broiler pan. Cook fish for 4 to 6 minutes; turn and cook for 3 to 5 minutes, or until fish is slightly firm to the touch.

4. Serve fish with mango relish.   *Makes 4 servings*

grilled spicy red snapper with jamaican mango & peach relish

entertaining
CHOICES

peanut butter fruit dip

  2 cups skim milk
½ cup light sour cream
  1 (3.4-ounce) package vanilla instant pudding and pie filling mix
  1 cup JIF® Reduced Fat Peanut Butter
⅓ cup sugar
    Apple and banana slices (or any fruit of your choice)

1. Combine milk, sour cream and pudding mix in medium bowl; whisk until smooth. Stir peanut butter until evenly mixed throughout; measure after stirring. Add peanut butter and sugar to pudding mixture; stir until well blended.

2. Serve dip with sliced apples and bananas. Store covered in refrigerator. *Makes 3 cups dip*

Tip: If dip becomes too thick, stir in additional milk.

Variation: Try stirring in ¼ cup Smucker's® Hot Fudge Ice Cream Topping to make a rich peanut butter and chocolate dessert dip.

elegant berry trifle

3 (3.4-ounce) packages vanilla pudding mix plus ingredients to prepare mixes
1½ teaspoons almond extract, divided
½ cup white grape juice
1 (12-ounce) loaf pound cake, cut into ½-inch slices
½ cup SMUCKER'S® Red Raspberry Preserves
½ cup SMUCKER'S® Blackberry Jam
1 cup whipping cream
1 tablespoon powdered sugar
1 teaspoon vanilla
8 crisp almond macaroon cookies, crushed, or ¼ cup toasted slivered almonds

1. Prepare pudding mixes according to package directions; cool. Blend in 1 teaspoon almond extract; set aside. Combine remaining ½ teaspoon extract with grape juice in small bowl; set aside.

2. Spread ¼ of pound cake slices with raspberry preserves and ¼ with blackberry jam; top each spread slice with unspread slice to form "sandwiches." Cut sandwiches into ¾-inch pieces. Reserve a few pieces for garnish; sprinkle remaining pieces with grape juice mixture.

3. To assemble trifle, spoon ⅓ of pudding into 6-cup dessert dish or trifle bowl. Alternate raspberry and blackberry cake pieces in pattern on pudding, using half of pieces. Repeat layers; top with remaining pudding. Refrigerate several hours.

4. Shortly before serving, whip cream with powdered sugar and vanilla until soft peaks form. Sprinkle crushed macaroons around edge of dish. Pipe rosettes or spoon dollops of whipped cream on top of trifle; garnish with reserved cake pieces.   *Makes 10 to 12 servings*

elegant berry trifle

CHOICES

spicy apricot chicken wings

2 pounds chicken wings
1 cup SMUCKER'S® Apricot Preserves
2 tablespoons cider vinegar
1 to 2 teaspoons hot pepper sauce
1 teaspoon chili powder
1 clove garlic, minced

1. Cut off and discard chicken wing tips. Cut each chicken wing in half at joint. Place wings in resealable plastic food storage bag; set aside.

2. Combine preserves, vinegar, hot pepper sauce (2 teaspoons for extra-hot sauce), chili powder and garlic in small bowl. Pour ½ cup sauce into plastic bag with chicken; seal bag. Marinate for at least 1 hour or overnight. Cover and refrigerate remaining sauce.

3. Place chicken wings on preheated grill. Discard marinade. Cook wings for 25 to 30 minutes.

4. Serve wings with remaining refrigerated sauce.

Make 8 to 10 servings

Tip

The sauce also works well with 1 pound uncooked large shrimp. Marinate the shrimp as directed in the above recipe. Grill the shrimp for about 5 minutes or until cooked through.

glazed meatballs

½ pound ground beef
¼ cup fine dry bread crumbs
¼ cup minced onion
 1 egg, beaten
 2 tablespoons milk
½ teaspoon salt
¼ teaspoon Worcestershire sauce
⅛ teaspoon black pepper
 2 tablespoons CRISCO® All-Vegetable Oil*
½ cup (6 ounces) chili sauce
½ cup SMUCKER'S® Grape Jelly

Or use your favorite Crisco Oil.

1. Combine first 8 ingredients in large bowl; mix well. Shape into 1-inch meatballs.

2. Cook in oil over medium heat for 10 to 15 minutes or until browned. Drain on paper towels.

3. Combine chili sauce and jelly in medium saucepan; stir well. Add meatballs; simmer 30 minutes, stirring occasionally. Serve in chafing dish. *Makes about 2½ dozen meatballs*

CHOICES

marinated chicken satay with peanut butter dipping sauce

CHICKEN AND MARINADE
- ½ cup Italian salad dressing
- 2 tablespoons JIF® Creamy Peanut Butter
- 1 pound boneless skinless chicken breasts, cut into ½×4-inch strips
- 10 to 12 wooden skewers (soak in warm water for 30 minutes prior to use)

DIPPING SAUCE
- ½ cup JIF® Creamy Peanut Butter
- ½ cup chopped fresh parsley or cilantro leaves
- 6 tablespoons water
- 3 tablespoons fresh lime juice
- 2 tablespoons reduced-sodium soy sauce
- 1 tablespoon honey
- 1 teaspoon sesame oil
- Pinch cayenne powder

1. Combine salad dressing and peanut butter in medium bowl; whisk until smooth. Place chicken strips in peanut butter mixture. Cover and marinate in refrigerator for 3 hours or overnight.

2. For dipping sauce, place all ingredients in blender; blend on medium-high until smooth.

3. Preheat broiler. Remove chicken from refrigerator. Thread 2 chicken strips onto each skewer. Arrange skewers on metal grill rack positioned over foil-lined baking pan. Broil skewers for 6 minutes; turn skewers over. Broil for another 4 to 6 minutes or until juices run clear and chicken is thoroughly cooked. Serve chicken skewers with dipping sauce, if desired.   *Make 3 to 4 servings*

Note: To grill, place skewered chicken on hot grill for 8 minutes, or until juices run clear.

marinated chicken satay with peanut butter dipping sauce

CHOICES

sautéed swordfish with cherry salsa

SALSA

   2 cups coarsely chopped fresh tomatoes
   1 cup coarsely chopped red bell pepper
   1 cup coarsely chopped green bell pepper
   ½ cup coarsely chopped onion
   ½ cup SMUCKER'S® Cherry Preserves
   ¼ cup minced jalapeño or other hot chili peppers*
   1 teaspoon hot pepper sauce
   ½ teaspoon salt

SWORDFISH

   3 to 4 tablespoons CRISCO® Vegetable Oil**
1½ pounds fresh swordfish, cut into 4 portions (about 1 inch thick)
   Salt and black pepper to taste

When handling chili peppers, be sure to wear rubber gloves and do not touch your face, nose, eyes or lips before thoroughly washing your hands.

**Or use your favorite Crisco Oil.*

1. Combine salsa ingredients in food processor; pulse 4 to 8 times or until salsa is slightly chunky.

2. Heat oil in heavy cast iron or nonstick skillet over medium-high heat. Lightly season swordfish with salt and pepper; place in skillet.

3. Cook swordfish for 5 to 7 minutes; turn and cook for 8 minutes longer or until swordfish is slightly firm to the touch.

4. Place swordfish on serving plates; top each slice with a few tablespoons of salsa.

Makes 4 servings

sautéed swordfish with cherry salsa

delectable
DESSERTS

chocolate fudge

1½ cups sugar
 1 cup marshmallow creme
½ cup evaporated milk
⅓ cup Reduced Fat JIF® Creamy Peanut Butter
½ teaspoon salt
 1 (6-ounce) package semisweet chocolate chips
 1 teaspoon vanilla

1. Grease 8-inch square baking pan.

2. Combine sugar, marshmallow creme, milk, peanut butter and salt in large saucepan. Stir constantly over low heat until blended and mixture comes to a boil.

3. Boil 5 minutes, stirring constantly. Remove from heat. Add chocolate chips; stir until well blended. Stir in vanilla.

4. Pour into prepared pan; cool. Cut into candy-sized pieces. Store in covered container.

Makes 1 to 1½ pounds fudge

Variation: For an even more decadent fudge, stir in ½ cup miniature marshmallows, crushed toffee or chopped nuts at the same time you add the vanilla.

DESSERTS

lemon raspberry cheesecake bars

CRUST
   ¾ CRISCO® Butter Flavor Stick or ¾ cup CRISCO® Butter Flavor
      Shortening plus additional for greasing
   ½ cup firmly packed brown sugar
1¼ cups PILLSBURY BEST® All-Purpose or Unbleached Flour
   1 cup uncooked oats
   ¼ teaspoon salt

FILLING
   ½ cup SMUCKER'S® Red Raspberry Jam
   2 (8-ounce) packages cream cheese, softened
   ¾ cup granulated sugar
   2 tablespoons PILLSBURY BEST® All-Purpose or Unbleached Flour
   2 eggs
   3 tablespoons lemon juice
   2 teaspoons grated lemon peel

1. Preheat oven to 350°F. Grease 13×9×2-inch baking pan with shortening.

2. For crust, combine ¾ cup shortening and brown sugar in large bowl. Beat at medium speed with electric mixer until well blended. Gradually add 1¼ cups flour, oats and salt, beating at low speed until well blended. Press onto bottom of prepared pan.

3. Bake at 350°F for 20 minutes or until lightly browned.

4. For filling, spoon jam immediately on hot crust. Spread carefully to cover.

5. Combine cream cheese, granulated sugar and 2 tablespoons flour in large bowl. Beat at low speed until well blended. Add eggs; beat until well blended. Add lemon juice and lemon peel; beat until smooth. Pour over raspberry layer.

6. Bake at 350°F for 25 minutes or until set. Remove pan to cooling rack; let cool to room temperature. Cut into 2×1½-inch bars. Cover and refrigerate. *Makes 3 dozen bars*

Pillsbury Best is a trademark of The Pillsbury Company, used under license.

lemon raspberry cheesecake bars

DESSERTS

bumpy highway cake

CAKE
CRISCO® No-Stick Cooking Spray
1 (14-ounce) can sweetened condensed milk (not evaporated milk), divided
1 CRISCO® Butter Flavor Stick or 1 cup CRISCO® Butter Flavor Shortening plus additional for greasing
1 cup granulated sugar
1 cup firmly packed light brown sugar
4 eggs
2 teaspoons vanilla
1 cup buttermilk
½ cup unsweetened cocoa powder
2½ cups PILLSBURY BEST® All-Purpose or Unbleached Flour
1 teaspoon baking soda
1 teaspoon ground cinnamon
½ teaspoon salt
1 cup hot water

FROSTING
½ cup powdered sugar
2 tablespoons CRISCO® Butter Flavor Stick or 2 tablespoons CRISCO® Butter Flavor Shortening
1 cup chopped nuts
½ cup miniature marshmallows, halved

DRIZZLE
⅓ cup SMUCKER'S® Chocolate Sundae Syrup

1. Preheat oven to 350°F. Grease 10-inch (12-cup) Bundt pan with cooking spray; flour lightly.

2. Measure ⅓ cup condensed milk for cake. Reserve remaining milk for frosting.

3. For cake, combine 1 cup shortening, granulated sugar, brown sugar, eggs, ⅓ cup condensed milk and vanilla in large bowl. Beat at medium speed of electric mixer until creamy. Add buttermilk and cocoa; beat until well blended.

4. Combine flour, baking soda, cinnamon and salt in medium bowl. Add to creamed mixture; beat at low speed until blended. Beat at medium speed 5 minutes. Stir in hot water with spoon just until blended. Do not overmix. (Batter will be thin.) Pour into prepared pan.

5. Bake at 350°F for 35 to 50 minutes or until top springs back when touched lightly in center or until toothpick inserted into center comes out clean. Do not overbake. Cool 10 minutes before removing from pan. Place cake, fluted side up, on serving plate. Cool 10 minutes.

6. For frosting, combine powdered sugar, ½ cup reserved condensed milk and 2 tablespoons shortening in medium bowl. Beat at high speed until glossy and of desired spreading consistency. Spread over warm cake. Sprinkle with nuts and marshmallows. Drizzle with chocolate syrup. Serve warm or cool completely.

Makes 1 (10-inch) bundt cake (12 to 16 servings)

DESSERTS

peanut butter kisses

1 cup granulated sugar
1 cup packed brown sugar
1 cup CRISCO® Shortening
1 cup JIF® Peanut Butter
2 eggs
¼ cup milk
2 teaspoons vanilla
3½ cups sifted PILLSBURY BEST® All-Purpose Flour
2 teaspoons baking soda
1 teaspoon salt
Additional granulated sugar
1 (11-ounce) package milk chocolate candies

1. Preheat oven to 375°F.

2. Combine granulated sugar, brown sugar, shortening and peanut butter in large bowl; beat until well blended. Add eggs, milk and vanilla; beat well.

3. Stir together flour, baking soda and salt in medium bowl; add to peanut butter mixture. Beat well.

4. Shape dough into 1-inch balls; roll in additional granulated sugar. Place on ungreased baking sheet.

5. Bake at 375°F for 8 minutes. Remove from oven. Press one milk chocolate candy into center of each warm cookie. Return to oven; bake 3 minutes longer.   *Makes 6 to 7 dozen cookies*

Pillsbury Best is a trademark of The Pillsbury Company, used under license.

DESSERTS

peanut butter marshmallow bars

½ CRISCO® Butter Flavor Stick or ½ cup CRISCO® Butter Flavor
  Shortening plus additional for greasing
½ cup JIF® Extra Crunchy Peanut Butter
¼ cup granulated sugar
¼ cup firmly packed light brown sugar
 1 egg
1¼ cups PILLSBURY BEST® All-Purpose Flour
 1 teaspoon baking powder
¼ teaspoon salt
½ cup JIF® Creamy Peanut Butter
 4 cups miniature marshmallows
½ cup chocolate flavored syrup

1. Preheat oven to 350°F. Grease 13×9×2-inch glass baking dish with shortening.

2. For cookie base, combine shortening, extra crunchy peanut butter, granulated sugar, brown sugar and egg in large bowl. Beat at medium speed of electric mixer until well blended.

3. Combine flour, baking powder and salt in medium bowl. Add gradually to creamed mixture at low speed. Beat until well blended. Cover and refrigerate 15 minutes.

4. Press chilled cookie base into prepared dish. Bake at 350°F for 20 minutes or until light brown. Do not overbake. Cool for 2 to 3 minutes.

5. For topping, place creamy peanut butter in microwave-safe measuring cup. Microwave at HIGH for 1 minute. Pour over baked surface. Spread to cover. Top with marshmallows. Drizzle chocolate syrup over marshmallows. Return to oven. Bake 5 minutes or until marshmallows are light brown. Do not overbake. Loosen from sides of dish with knife. Remove dish to cooling rack. Cool completely. Cut with sharp greased knife into 2¼×2-inch bars.   *Makes 2 dozen bars*

Pillsbury Best is a trademark of The Pillsbury Company, used under license.

peanut butter marshmallow bars

DESSERTS

peanut butter and jelly crispies

½ CRISCO® Butter Flavor Stick or ½ cup CRISCO® Butter Flavor
    Shortening plus additional for greasing
½ cup JIF® Crunchy Peanut Butter
½ cup granulated sugar
½ cup firmly packed light brown sugar
 1 egg
1¼ cups PILLSBURY BEST® All-Purpose or Unbleached Flour
½ teaspoon baking powder
½ teaspoon baking soda
¼ teaspoon salt
 2 cups crisp rice cereal
    Honey roasted peanuts, finely chopped (optional)
    SMUCKER'S® Jelly, any flavor

1. Preheat oven to 375°F. Grease 13×9×2-inch baking pan with shortening. Place wire rack on countertop for cooling bars.

2. Combine ½ cup shortening, peanut butter, granulated sugar and brown sugar in large bowl. Beat at medium speed of electric mixer until well blended. Beat in egg.

3. Combine flour, baking powder, baking soda and salt in medium bowl. Add gradually to creamed mixture at low speed. Beat until well blended. Add cereal; stir just until blended. Press into prepared pan. Sprinkle with nuts, if desired.

4. Score dough into 2¼×2-inch bars. Press thumb in center of each. Fill indentation with ¼ to ½ teaspoon jelly.

5. Bake at 375°F for 12 to 15 minutes or until golden brown. Do not overbake. Remove pan to wire rack. Cool for 2 to 3 minutes. Cut into bars. Cool completely. *Makes about 2 dozen bars*

Pillsbury Best is a trademark of The Pillsbury Company, used under license.

DESSERTS

decadent peanut butter pie

1 prepared chocolate graham cracker pie crust
1 egg white, beaten
1 cup JIF® Creamy Peanut Butter
1 (8-ounce) package cream cheese, at room temperature
½ cup sugar
4 cups non-dairy whipped topping, divided
¼ cup heavy cream
½ cup plus 1 tablespoon SMUCKER'S® Hot Fudge Ice Cream
    Topping
2 tablespoons finely chopped dry-roasted peanuts (optional)

1. Preheat oven to 375°F. Brush crust with beaten egg white. Bake for 5 minutes. Remove crust from oven; set aside to cool.

2. Combine peanut butter, cream cheese and sugar in medium bowl. Gently fold in 2 cups whipped topping, ½ cup at a time (a few creamy streaks will remain in mixture). Spoon mixture into cooled pie shell. Smooth top using spatula; make ½-inch ridge around edge to keep topping from sliding off. Refrigerate.

3. Place cream in microwave-safe bowl; heat on HIGH for 1 minute or just until boiling. Stir hot fudge ice cream topping into cream until completely melted. Reserve 1 tablespoon mixture. Gently spread remaining mixture onto chilled pie. Refrigerate pie again until nearly firm, about 1 hour.

4. Spread remaining 2 cups whipped topping over top of chilled pie, covering fudge topping layer. Drizzle with reserved chocolate mixture; sprinkle with peanuts. Refrigerate until serving time.

Makes 10 servings

decadent peanut butter pie

irresistible peanut butter cookies

1¼ cups firmly packed light brown sugar
¾ cup JIF® Creamy Peanut Butter
½ CRISCO® Butter Flavor Stick or ½ cup CRISCO® Butter Flavor Shortening
3 tablespoons milk
1 tablespoon vanilla
1 egg
1¾ cups PILLSBURY BEST® All-Purpose Flour
¾ teaspoon baking soda
¾ teaspoon salt

1. Preheat oven to 375°F. Place sheets of foil on countertop for cooling cookies.

2. Combine brown sugar, peanut butter, ½ cup shortening, milk and vanilla in large bowl. Beat at medium speed of electric mixer until well blended. Add egg. Beat just until blended.

3. Combine flour, baking soda and salt in medium bowl. Add to creamed mixture at low speed. Mix just until blended.

4. Drop dough by rounded measuring tablespoonfuls 2 inches apart onto ungreased baking sheet. Flatten slightly in crisscross pattern with tines of fork.

5. Bake one baking sheet at a time at 375°F for 7 to 8 minutes, or until set and just beginning to brown. Do not overbake. Cool 2 minutes on baking sheet. Remove cookies to foil to cool completely.

Makes about 3 dozen cookies

Pillsbury Best is a trademark of The Pillsbury Company, used under license.

irresistible peanut butter cookies

DESSERTS

chocolate raspberry cake

 4 (1-ounce) squares unsweetened chocolate
¼ cup water
½ cup butter or margarine, cut into small pieces
½ cup sugar
 3 eggs, separated
⅓ cup PILLSBURY BEST® All-Purpose Flour
½ cup SMUCKER'S® Red Raspberry Preserves or Apricot Preserves
   Chocolate shavings
   Fresh raspberries

1. Preheat oven to 325°F. Grease and flour 2 (8-inch) round cake pans; set aside.

2. Melt chocolate with water in medium saucepan over low heat, stirring constantly. Add butter; stir until completely melted. Remove from heat and blend in sugar; cool.

3. Add egg yolks to chocolate mixture, one at a time, beating well after each addition. Add flour; blend well. Beat egg whites in clean bowl until stiff but not dry; fold into chocolate mixture. Pour into prepared cake pans.

4. Bake at 325°F for 25 minutes or until toothpick inserted into centers of cakes comes out clean. Remove cakes from pans and cool completely on wire racks.

5. Heat preserves in small saucepan until melted. Spread half of preserves on 1 cake layer. Top with second cake layer; spread with remaining preserves. Garnish with chocolate shavings and raspberries.

Makes 12 to 15 servings

Note: For chocolate shavings, melt 1 to 2 ounces of semisweet chocolate. Spread melted chocolate in thick layer on baking sheet; refrigerate until set. Scrape with metal spatula held at 45° angle to produce shavings and curls. Chill or freeze shavings until ready to use.

Pillsbury Best is a trademark of The Pillsbury Company, used under license.

METRIC CONVERSION CHART

VOLUME MEASUREMENTS (dry)

$1/8$ teaspoon = 0.5 mL
$1/4$ teaspoon = 1 mL
$1/2$ teaspoon = 2 mL
$3/4$ teaspoon = 4 mL
1 teaspoon = 5 mL
1 tablespoon = 15 mL
2 tablespoons = 30 mL
$1/4$ cup = 60 mL
$1/3$ cup = 75 mL
$1/2$ cup = 125 mL
$2/3$ cup = 150 mL
$3/4$ cup = 175 mL
1 cup = 250 mL
2 cups = 1 pint = 500 mL
3 cups = 750 mL
4 cups = 1 quart = 1 L

VOLUME MEASUREMENTS (fluid)

1 fluid ounce (2 tablespoons) = 30 mL
4 fluid ounces ($1/2$ cup) = 125 mL
8 fluid ounces (1 cup) = 250 mL
12 fluid ounces ($1 1/2$ cups) = 375 mL
16 fluid ounces (2 cups) = 500 mL

WEIGHTS (mass)

$1/2$ ounce = 15 g
1 ounce = 30 g
3 ounces = 90 g
4 ounces = 120 g
8 ounces = 225 g
10 ounces = 285 g
12 ounces = 360 g
16 ounces = 1 pound = 450 g

DIMENSIONS

$1/16$ inch = 2 mm
$1/8$ inch = 3 mm
$1/4$ inch = 6 mm
$1/2$ inch = 1.5 cm
$3/4$ inch = 2 cm
1 inch = 2.5 cm

OVEN TEMPERATURES

250°F = 120°C
275°F = 140°C
300°F = 150°C
325°F = 160°C
350°F = 180°C
375°F = 190°C
400°F = 200°C
425°F = 220°C
450°F = 230°C

BAKING PAN SIZES

Utensil	Size in Inches/Quarts	Metric Volume	Size in Centimeters
Baking or Cake Pan (square or rectangular)	8×8×2	2 L	20×20×5
	9×9×2	2.5 L	23×23×5
	12×8×2	3 L	30×20×5
	13×9×2	3.5 L	33×23×5
Loaf Pan	8×4×3	1.5 L	20×10×7
	9×5×3	2 L	23×13×7
Round Layer Cake Pan	8×1½	1.2 L	20×4
	9×1½	1.5 L	23×4
Pie Plate	8×1¼	750 mL	20×3
	9×1¼	1 L	23×3
Baking Dish or Casserole	1 quart	1 L	—
	1½ quart	1.5 L	—
	2 quart	2 L	—